Dorothea's Eyes

DOROTHEA LANGE
PHOTOGRAPHS
THE TRUTH

Barb Rosenstock

Illustrations by
Gérard DuBois

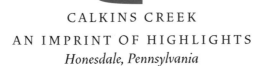

CALKINS CREEK

AN IMPRINT OF HIGHLIGHTS
Honesdale, Pennsylvania

Calkins Creek
An Imprint of Highlights
815 Church Street
Honesdale, Pennsylvania 18431

Printed in Malaysia
ISBN: 978-1-62979-208-8
Library of Congress Control Number: 2015946898

First edition

Book design by Anahid Hamparian
Production by Sue Cole
The text of this book is set in Stempel Schneidler.
The illustrations are done in acrylic on paper and digital.

10 9 8 7 6 5 4 3 2 1

For my grandfather

—BR

To my sister, with love

—GD

Acknowledgments

Thanks to Mitra Abbaspour, Adjunct Professor, The Cooper Union; Gray Brechin, Project Scientist, The Living New Deal Project at U.C. Berkeley; Elizabeth Cronin, Assistant Curator at The New York Public Library; Marcia Eymann, Executive Director of the Sacramento History Museum; and Sally Stein, Professor Emeritus, U.C.-Irvine, for their review of the manuscript and artwork.

Dorothea Lange Photograph Credits

*"This is the way it is.
Look at it!
Look at it!"*

—Dorothea Lange

Dorothea opens her grey-green eyes.

They are special **eyes**.

They see what others miss. . . .

Dimpled shadows scattering an orange peel.

Swirled-pattern pricks in a walnut sewing table.

Repeating rectangles of New Jersey row houses.

Dorothea loves faces! Mother's curved cheeks.

Father's angled jaw. Grandmother's pursed lips.

Baby brother's squat nose.

When Dorothea looks at faces, it's like she's hugging the world.

When she is seven, Dorothea gets very sick.

Every feverish muscle aches; soon she can't move at all.

She sees doctors, hears scary words. **Polio. Paralyze.**

No one talks to her. *Can't they see me?* she wonders.

Dorothea sees everything.

Dorothea soon feels better, but her right foot flops at the end of a forever-withered leg. Kids call her "Limpy," and she wants to hide. Mother whispers, "Walk as well as you can," and Dorothea pretends to be invisible.

She blends into the background as her parents fight about money. When she is twelve, Father leaves forever. Mother finds a job in a city library. Every weekday, Dorothea and her mother take the ferry to New York. Mother works long hours and Dorothea is the new girl in a school full of poor immigrants.

Different.   Lonely.

Waiting for Mother at the library after school,
Dorothea spies into crowded tenements where fathers,
home from peddling, read newspapers, and mothers
wash dishes, clothes, and babies in rusty sinks—
happy and sad mixed together.

Dorothea pretends she's **invisible** all the time.
Her eyes work better that way. She skips school
to wander the city, walking alone through
tough crowds and blowing trash.

Watchful.   **Curious.**

Dorothea sees with her eyes *and* her heart.

When she is almost grown, Dorothea surprises everyone.
"I'm going to be a photographer!" Her family is shocked;
Dorothea's never held a camera! Taking pictures of strangers?
Mixing dangerous chemicals? Carrying heavy equipment?
It . . . it isn't ladylike!

Eighteen-year-old Dorothea doesn't care what's proper; she wants to show the world what she sees. She limps up the stairs to photographers' studios, rings doorbells, and asks for work. Dorothea answers phones, makes appointments, mounts photographs—excited to learn more.

One photographer gives Dorothea an old camera.
She learns its parts. Lens. Shutter. Aperture. She
learns about different-sized cameras—some use
heavy glass plates bigger than Dorothea's head.

She helps another photographer build a darkroom
from a chicken coop—blocking light, testing water
temperatures, and drying negatives. Alone in the
darkroom's amber glow, she studies the wet printing
paper while faces appear in black and white.

Dorothea loves faces!

Her restless eyes need to see new places. At twenty-three, Dorothea sets off on a trip around the world, first traveling west by train. When all her money is stolen in San Francisco, she stays in that city, gets a job developing photographs, and starts her own portrait studio.

When Dorothea disappears behind the camera, she captures lovely faces on film. In a flash, all the richest families in California want portraits by Dorothea Lange. She makes money and friends; she marries, starts a family. Outside, she belongs. Inside, she wonders.

Am I using my eyes and *my heart?*

One day, through her studio window, Dorothea's eyes trace the path of a man wandering in the street below. He's come to the city for work, but can't find a job. No one can. The stock market has crashed. Banks and shops have closed. Newspapers call it the Great Depression.

She sees another man and another. One by one they stop at the corner. **Sad. Lost.** No one in the street notices. Dorothea's eyes can't look away. She grabs a camera and heads outside the studio into the world.

In a crowd of men waiting for bread, one face turns from the others. Dorothea focuses on that lone man, a battered cup in his hand.

She takes photo after photo. She hangs them on her studio walls. Her friends don't understand. No one takes portraits of poor people!

Dorothea's heart won't let her stop.

Dorothea leaves her comfortable life and takes her camera on the road. She scans dirt lanes, peers down back paths, and squints up broken steps. Fathers stoop in fields, working for pennies. Mothers nurse sick children, lying thirsty in makeshift tents. Whole families live in jalopies—blown out by the dust storms wracking the land.

Dorothea limps toward these hungry strangers.

Her heart knows all about people the world ignores.

She asks gentle questions. *Where are you from?*
How old are the children? Later, *Can I take photographs?*
They are ashamed. They are **invisible.** Dorothea understands.
She loves their faces! And their faces tell her camera the truth.
They are good people in real trouble.

Many days, Dorothea struggles. She's tired. Her leg hurts
always. For five years, in twenty-two states, Dorothea drags
through fields, climbs on cars, and crouches in the dirt to
photograph people the world can't see. The jobless.
The hungry. The homeless.

Newspapers and magazines publish these pictures.
Dorothea's eyes won't let the country look away.
Her photographs help convince the government to provide
parents with work, children with food, and families with
safe, clean homes.

The truth, seen with love, becomes Dorothea's art.

And long after her time, Dorothea's photographs still tell the truth. That each person is special. That people need each other. That life is happy and sad mixed together.

Dorothea's eyes help us see with our hearts.

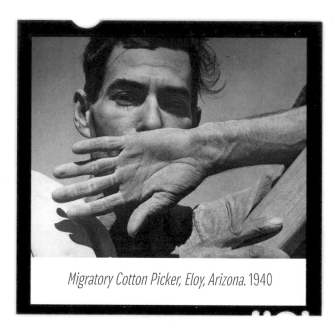

Migratory Cotton Picker, Eloy, Arizona. 1940

Destitute pea pickers in California. Mother of seven children.
Age thirty-two. Nipomo, California.
Migrant Mother. 1936

Mississippi Delta Negro Children. 1936

Ex-Slave with a Long Memory. 1938

White Angel Bread Line, San Francisco. 1933

Woman of the High Plains. 1938

"I've never not been sure that I was a photographer, any more than you would not be sure that you were yourself." —Dorothea Lange

Dorothea Lange was an important American photographer. Her image *Migrant Mother* is one of the most famous, most reproduced photographs in history. Lange was the only woman in the earliest group of photographers hired by President Franklin D. Roosevelt's New Deal government to document the people and events of the Great Depression. She helped develop a style called documentary photography ("images that realistically depict actual situations . . . often of sociological or political import"). Lange also wrote factual, heartfelt captions that captured the lives of the people she photographed.

Lange was the first woman awarded the prestigious Guggenheim Fellowship and one of the few photographers who documented Japanese internment camps during World War II. The U.S. Army impounded her powerful, critical images of the camps for years; many were first published in 2006.

Lange taught photography at the California School of Fine Arts and cofounded the photography magazine *Aperture*. Her work was featured in Edward Steichen's important 1955 photography exhibit, *The Family of Man*, at New York's Museum of Modern Art, and in *Life* magazine. Her photographs influenced John Steinbeck's novel *The Grapes of Wrath* and Lange is listed in *The 100 Most Influential Women of All Time* by Deborah Felder. Despite decades of ill health from ulcers and post-polio syndrome, Dorothea Lange continued photographing faces—from strangers on five continents to her adored grandchildren—until the end of her life.

Many of Dorothea Lange's photographs are held at the National Archives and can be accessed at their website (archives.gov), in the "Prints & Photographs" online catalog at the Library of Congress website (loc.gov/pictures), or at Yale University's Photogrammar site (photogrammar.yale.edu). Prints of Dorothea's photographs are in the collections of the Oakland Museum of California; the San Francisco Museum of Modern Art; the New York Public Library; the Museum of Modern Art (MoMA) in New York City; the Library of Congress in Washington, DC; the Nelson-Atkins Museum of Art in Kansas City; the Cleveland Museum of Art; and the Harry Ransom Center at the University of Texas at Austin. I hope you will look at Dorothea's photographs with your eyes and your heart.

"I knew how to keep an expression . . . that would draw no attention, so no one would look at me. I have used that my whole life in photography. . . . I can turn it on and off. If I don't want anyone to see me I can make the kind of face so eyes go off me. . . . I was never obviously there." —Dorothea Lange

Selected Bibliography

Gordon, Linda. *Dorothea Lange: A Life Beyond Limits*. New York: W.W. Norton, 2009.

Greene, Philip, and Richard Moore, dir. *Dorothea Lange: Part One: Under the Trees; Part Two: The Closer for Me*. KQED Film Unit Production, June 1965. Online at diva.sfsu.edu/collections/sfbatv/bundles/191509 and diva.sfsu.edu/collections/sfbatv/bundles/191510.

Lange, Dorothea. Interview by Richard K. Doud. *Oral history interview with Dorothea Lange, New York City, May 22, 1964*. Archives of American Art, Smithsonian Institution. aaa.si.edu/collections/interviews/oral-history-interview-dorothea-lange-11757.

Lange, Dorothea. Interview by Suzanne Riess. *Dorothea Lange: The Making of A Documentary Photographer*. Berkeley: Regional Oral History Office, Bancroft Library, University of California, 1968.

Meltzer, Milton. *Dorothea Lange: A Photographer's Life*. New York: Farrar, Straus & Giroux, 1978.

Ohrn, Karin Becker. *Dorothea Lange and the Documentary Tradition*. Baton Rouge: Louisiana State University Press, 1980.

Spirn, Anne Whiston. *Daring to Look: Dorothea Lange's Photographs and Reports from the Field*. Chicago: The University of Chicago Press, 2008.

Sources for Quotations

"This is the way . . ." Greene & Moore, Part Two; *The Closer for Me*, 26:18.

"I've never not been . . ." Lange, *The Making of a Documentary Photographer*, p. 36.

"images that realistically . . ." Lynch-Johnt, B., and M. Perkins, *Illustrated Dictionary of Photography*, Buffalo, NY: Amherst Media, 2008, p. 29.

"I knew how to keep . . ." Lange, *The Making of a Documentary Photographer*, p. 16.

For Further Reading

Partridge, Elizabeth. *Dorothea Lange: Grab a Hunk of Lightning*. San Francisco: Chronicle Books, 2013.

Partridge, Elizabeth. *Restless Spirit: The Life and Work of Dorothea Lange*. New York: Viking, 1998.

Sandler, Martin. *America Through the Lens: Photographers who Changed the Nation*. New York: Henry Holt, 2005.

Timeline

1895 Born Dorothea Margaretta Nutzhorn to Heinrich (Henry) Nutzhorn and Johanna (Joan) Lange at 1041 Bloomfield Street, Hoboken, New Jersey.

1901 Brother, Henry Martin (Martin), is born.

1902 Contracts polio, is left with two different-sized feet and a limp from a damaged leg. Wears steel braces and a different-sized boot on her right leg for an unknown period of time. Attends elementary school in Hoboken.

1907 Henry Nutzhorn leaves the family home. Dorothea and her mother and brother move in with Dorothea's maternal grandmother, Sophie Lange. Joan supports the family by working at the Chatham Square Branch of the New York Public Library. Dorothea attends Intermediate P.S. 62 on the Lower East Side.

1913 Dorothea graduates from Wadleigh High School for Girls in Harlem. Decides to be a photographer.

1914–1917 At family's insistence, Dorothea attends teacher training school. Also takes photography classes from Clarence White at Columbia University and works in the studios of portrait photographers including Arnold Genthe and Aram Kazanjian. First portrait commission for the wealthy Brokaw family.

1918 In January, Dorothea intends to travel around the world with a friend, Florence (Fronsie) Ahlstrom. Starts out by train—stopping in Louisiana, Texas, and New Mexico. Their money is stolen and they are stranded in San Francisco, California. Dorothea takes her mother's maiden name, Lange. Works at a department store developing photos, meets many people in the arts community, and starts a portrait studio.

1920 Marries the landscape painter Maynard Dixon.

1925 Son, Daniel Rhodes Dixon, is born.

1928 Son, John Eaglefeather Dixon, is born.

1929 *Stock Market Crash, start of the Great Depression.*

1933 Photographs *White Angel Bread Line*, a picture of displaced men in San Francisco's streets.

1934 First exhibition of Dorothea's photographs in Oakland, California. Her work first appears in magazines.

1935 Divorces Maynard Dixon and marries economics professor Paul Taylor.

1935–1939 Travels the country for the U.S. Farm Security Administration (FSA). Photographs *Mississippi Delta Negro Children* near Vicksburg, Mississippi, and *Ditched, Stalled and Stranded* in San Joaquin Valley, California.

1936 In Nipomo, California, photographs *Migrant Mother*, the most widely known documentary photograph of the twentieth century. Over 20,000 pounds of food are shipped to the pea farm where the picture was taken.

1937–1938 Photographs *Ex-Slave with a Long Memory*, Alabama.

1938 Photographs *Woman of the High Plains*, Texas Panhandle.

1939 Publishes a book of photos, *An American Exodus*, with text by Paul Taylor. Photographs *Colored Tenant* in Chatham County, North Carolina, and *Mother & Baby of Family on the Road (Coca Cola Baby Bottle)* in Tulelake, California.

1940 Exhibits photographs at the Museum of Modern Art (MoMA) in New York. Suffers from bleeding ulcers, gastritis, debilitating fatigue, and muscle pain. Photographs *Migratory Cotton Picker* in Eloy, Arizona.

1941 Awarded Guggenheim Foundation fellowship for excellence in photography.

1941 *Preparations for war end the Great Depression. U.S. enters World War II in December.*

1942–1945 Documents war effort, including Japanese internment, for the U.S. government. Photographs *One Nation Indivisible* and *Enforcement of Executive Order 9066* in California.

1945 *World War II ends.*

1945–1951 Stops work due to ongoing health issues, now known as post-polio syndrome.

1951 Returns to photography. First grandchild born.

1952 Photographs *First Born*. Founds *Aperture* magazine with Ansel Adams, Minor White, Barbara Morgan, and Beaumont and Nancy Newhall.

1952 Works with Ansel Adams for *Life* magazine on *Three Mormon Towns*, published in 1954.

1954 Travels to Ireland on assignment for *Life* and *Irish Country People*, published in 1955.

1955 Works on *Public Defender*, a photo essay of daily life of court system. Dorothea's photographs included in *Family of Man*, a photography exhibition developed at MoMA that will tour the world for eight years and be seen by over nine million people.

1958–1962 Travels with Paul Taylor through Asia, South America, and Egypt, taking photographs.

1964 Organizes a major retrospective of her work to open at MoMA in 1966.

1965 Diagnosed with cancer of the esophagus. Dies October 11 in San Francisco.